THE ORCHID KEEPER

First published in 2006 by
The Dedalus Press
13 Moyclare Road
Baldoyle
Dublin 13
Ireland

www.dedaluspress.com

ISBN 1 904556 53 1

Dedalus Press titles are represented in North America
by Syracuse University Press, Inc., 621 Skytop Road,
Suite 110, Syracuse, New York 13244, and in the UK by
Central Books, 99 Wallis Road, London E9 5LN

Printed and bound in the UK by Lightning Source, 6 Precedent
Drive, Rooksley, Milton Keynes MK13 8PR

Design and typesetting by Pat Boran
Cover Image © David Freund / iStockphoto

The Dedalus Press receives financial assistance from
An Chomhairle Ealaíon / The Arts Council, Ireland.

THE ORCHID KEEPER

Paul Perry

ACKNOWLEDGEMENTS

Grateful acknowledgement is made to the editors of the following in which a number of these poems originally appeared or were broadcast: *The Texas Review, Poetry Ireland Review, Cork Literary Review, Poetry Salzburg, The Red Wheelbarrow, Abridged* and *Radio North West*, in conjunction with Scríobh Literary Festival, Sligo.

With thanks to the staff at the University of Ulster, in particular Frankie Sewell, John Gillespie and Robert Welch, and to the Rathlin Island Co-Operative Society who provided a residency during which some of these poems were written.

The author wishes to acknowledge receipt of a Bursary in Literature from the Arts Council / An Chomhairle Ealaíon, 2005.

for Aoife, le grá

i.m. Frances Quinn (1914—2006)

Contents

The Seals at Mill Bay, Rathlin   1
Wintering   3
Ode to a Car Crash   5
The Surfers of Portstewart   8
the boy with the kite   10
Fire of Stones   12
Ingredients for a Childhood Saturday   14
Lullaby, Dublin   16

✳

Towing an Iceberg to Belfast   21
Mêtro   25
Ode to a Badger   27
Prayer   30
Waiting   32
Longford, the Wind   34
my last poem   37

✳

The Lady with the Coronet of Jasmine   41

✳

Map Lover   53
Thoughts Concerning the Duration of Exile   55
A Letter from Perfect   57
Sunday in Belize   59
Variation on the word 'love'   61
on the avenue of the portal of angels # 7   63

The Orchid Keeper

The Seals at Mill Bay, Rathlin

Dark black and brown and grey
dappled pelts soaking,
lazing and luxuriating in the sun,
still and stretching,
fatty sculptures, sea-made,
salt-nourished, below the disused
kelp store. Bladder-wrack
and long tangle drying in the sun.
A rusted anchor lodged
into the soil beside briny
black lobster pots. They lounge
and bathe and buoy themselves up
to watch, caretakers among
the throng of building.
The sun's light dispersing,
mottled on the water, shimmering
like the cobweb on the windowsill,
holding fast its thin frayed
filaments set shining below
a trinity of windmills. Barking,
majestic mythical creatures,

I imagine the lost diver among you,

his friends' false skins discarded,
slung over the harbour railings
like seals who've left their bodies
to become seducing humans.
Wet suits disembodied,
masks and breathing apparatus,
fins and snorkels laid out.

The wreck he dived into empty,
the oxygen canisters empty,
among the black-eyed dreamers
his lungs empty,

but a seal's heart is full of love

which is perhaps what makes me
marvel at their watchful ways
and the perfect manner in which
they inhabit their bodies and dive
into the water which has carried
them to us and us to them.

Wintering

That was my last year in Florida,
illegal and thinking of marriage
as one way to stay. Sleepless nights
of argument and indecision. And

to keep us going I worked a cash job
at an orchid farm. Long hours
in the sun, poor in paradise, the heat
on my back, drilling for a living.

I worked with a Mexican.
My man Victor, the orchid keeper
called him, friendly and amused
at the affluent couples who came

to purchase the rich, ornate dreams.
We buried a dead owl together.
I remember that. And my body
aching in the sun. Floating home to arguments.

What we were doing I was told
was wintering. Getting ready
for the cold, its indiscretion, its disregard.
Nailing sheets of plastic onto a wooden

frame, hammering, drilling,
to protect the fragile flowers
and their steel interiors, their
engineered hearts and worth.

That is already a long time ago.
Its contradictions apparent.

Wintering in sunshine. The past
still growing towards the light.

I think of them now as some sort
of emblem of that past, ghostly
orchids shedding their petals,
as we winter here ourselves,

batten down the hatches and wait
for whatever storm is coming, whatever
calamity the cold has to offer us
in the same way the orchids do,

I suppose, waiting through winter
to emerge with budding, fantastical
insistence, to wake and remind us:
be nothing less than amazed.

Ode to a Car Crash

part of the field
it breathes at night
moves a grassy beast
home of grub and worm

victory for wild things
a vision of the future
imagine the driver concussed
thrown from the vehicle

intoxicated   bewildered
walking away from the site
the midden now
with a shake of the head

and a dismissive wave of the hand
years later the doors
are rusted unrecognizable
the wheels are gone

but the other driver
shadow driver ghost driver
some days in the night light
you'll find him still

clutching the steering wheel
as if he could take the vehicle
from danger at the crucial last moment
other days he's smoking a cigarette

invisible in the dusty sunshine
as a couple from the city
resettle into the countryside
circling his car's altar

he can never seem to leave it
he has the resigned look of the damned
not that he does not care
for his small cemetery

a caretaker a gardener of sorts
the soil grows the car sinks further
the ants make it home
a scrawny white cat hides from the rain

some days two teenagers kiss
in the back seat
the ghost driver watches shaking his head
what can he do

the boot is full of old clothes
but nothing goes to waste
one beggar who found the calamity
took himself a coat he still wears today

before long ... what's in a lifetime
the engine is removed
transplanted to another vehicle
at least part of it

one which swerves its way
around corners in another county
the doors are taken
the seats removed

the glass is spread like fallow seed
its only contribution
to the growth
a glimmer and twitch of light

one day when the surviving driver
turns this bend again he shivers

the car he can't recognize
doesn't see it's submerged

the memory is faint was it here
what turns his blood cold
and pushes his foot
onto the accelerator

is the man standing like a negative
all light on the side of the road
as if he had been waiting
like an old friend

his arm outstretched his thumb
pointing all the way to eternity

The Surfers of Portstewart

before the sun sets its great crimson eye
drawing you to look upon its alchemical grace

the surfers of Portstewart take flight like some
mythical fleet gliding over the waves

which then cover them in ceremonial gloss
as they go down into the depths

to resurface an age away their heads
popping out of the water like eager seals

I watch them all day and all day I've talked
to no one but myself let's just say I stayed

not here but back where we started our trip
settled down if you like maybe I'd have met

someone lost as you would have it
lost to another life and no longer playing

the game which makes me wonder
what possible lives we could have had

can have remember the laughter
the monkey-business in the R&B bar

or the Akka tribesman plying his trade
who no matter what he held up for our inspection

a bracelet a scales to measure opium
lisped the word *beautiful* with such unique

and phonic idiosyncrasy *beautiful*
that everything from then on

was just that: beautiful like Yung
and the look of wonder and hopelessness

no I correct you helplessness in your eyes
when you looked at her something I'd never seen

in you before so Xian what does it mean
to live out our days among strangers

another world away I'm not making any plans
I don't know where I'll be come twelve months

but I wanted to tell you this:
all day I've talked to no one but myself

and watched the surfers of Portstewart
they are the magic in my day

with their devotional patience
sitting on their boards waiting

waiting for the right wave
the wave that will take them there

where they were going
where they were always going

the boy with the kite

three cars are parked on the beach
a dog is running to and from the shore

chasing the tide out and scampering
away as it returns lovers walk with lazy steps

a girl with ponytails dances with two
handfuls of sand but the boy with the kite

sees none of it not even the sea
blue and green and black and moving

his gaze is turned skyward where a kite
a flame moves like an ancient dancer

a soul on a string waving and flinching
and diving like a frantic seagull into the unknown

all day people have fished and surfed
walked and believed in all manner

of miracle cars ice cream the resurrection
of the body but for the boy with the kite

there is only one prayer he doesn't hear
the dog bark he doesn't see the dropping sun

or hear the sound of night like an alarm
bell ringing over and over he's a lone dancer

a devotee to the beauty of flight
an admirer to the ballet of aeronautics

he can keep it there the kite still
like a humming bird so you can't even see

its wings fluttering at speed he they the boy
with the kite the boy *and* the kite

are a poem in the making and when he
walks away in the sky above him

in its eternal blueness the kite pivots and burns

Fire of Stones

smooth to the touch
and dark like the eyes of a dead cat

did I say cat
I meant brother

smooth smooth
smooth enough to soothe

and clean a wound
almost

found in a fish
that lived after

you had cut
its gut and taken

those black jewels
from inside

found in water
cold and clean

deep water salt water
off the island

where nobody lives
but ghosts with warning voices

heavy stones small
stones seven stones

for wishing stones
to trust and heat

stones for your bidding
but not to be sold

hidden in soil
or pillows

wrecking stones
hell stones

gall stones
kidney stones

black night time
sold your soul stones

dream stones
rubbing stones

worried disappearing
finger stones

swallowed like the flames
they light

flint and bone stones
sharp enough to cut a man

like you

Ingredients for a Childhood Saturday

If you grit your teeth
and search for scrap wood
by the market, trounce

some wooden carts,
suffer splinters in the hands,
return home to find a saw,

rusted in the shed,
unused. Slide its flaked
old smile across a fist

of rock. Cut to
arms length. Two notches
at the bottom end,

three in front. Run back
through the market.
Stop, thump the dead discarded

pig's head. Load the black
rubber rings. Crouch down
by the river and wait.

Take aim and fire.
If you are quarry
to the gang next door

lay low, hide,
play dumb and for god's sake
say

nothing of your whereabouts
to the buddha of insomnia,
the owl, or his friend,

otherwise known as judas, the crow.

Lullaby, Dublin

the rivers are rising
I wish I were fluent
in the language you speak
but mine is a mouth

full of teeth a mouth full
of blood and broken teeth
a night without dreams
is like a life unlived

I imagine
snails clustered on a driftwood fence
a sticky orgy bud burst
besting unfolding horse-chestnuts

I woke reciting a poem
a dreampoem for you
waiting to be written
but the words washed away

like a shape in sand washed over
your face in my hands
or crabs crawling
from their harbour walls

someone is after you
you're running scared
through alleys
and out of the city

over rocks and water
how many times have you
had this dream of me
waking to the thought of your body

my words
are like bones buried
or breaking on hilltops
a fire in the distance

listen
rivers are rising
the night is slipping away
with buskers and tourists

pigeons radios rubbish
guards cold swans on the grand canal
portobello traffic double deckers
people walking late night

newsagents cheap red wine talk
wet silver birches shivering
traffic lights changing no traffic
empty roads regrets and prayers

the quays and conversations with the self
laughter phonecalls chipper
front shutters closing
onions in the wind

bedraggled priest with bunch of roses
secular misgivings bus
shelter smashed old walls
falling headlines in the gutter

parked cars dark houses
taxis speeding goodbye
closed doors song of the old
hoarse night harbour storms

gossip and suburban insomnia
romanian requests for coins
and a gentle rain and roads
the golden mosque and fires

lit in a field sirens voices
in the wind the body of christ
and pubs clapping closed eyes
fitful sleep and seagulls

rain falling a smile
yours a small kiss pressed
to the hands
like a gift

Towing an Iceberg to Belfast
for Rita Duffy

On the tip of her tongue

She's ...

Don't think of melting

Pools along the way
A river

Think swimmers

Shipbuilding

On the long finger

She's ...

Don't say it

Stop making sense

She's ...

Towing an iceberg to Belfast

By a horse and cart

In wheelbarrows

A berg
A mountain
A mountain of ice

Read:

All poetry is performance
All poetry is L=A=N=G=U=A=G=E

Not *the* iceberg
An iceberg

Blue and …

By dreams
With dreams
In dreams
Amen

She's …

Towing an iceberg to Belfast

And gladly

To return

Return the scene of the crime
To its …

She's …

Towing an iceberg to Belfast

On the back
Of an old Morris Minor

An exploded artefact of sorts
From the Falls

We'll all be there
When she's coming 'round the mountain
Coming round
The mountain of ice
            The ice berg
                        We'll all be there

Takes time
            And money
Poets with money
            Pleased to meet you

The latest craze
            It's the thing to do
It's what we wanted
            But never knew

It's like how come
            We never thought
Of this before
            It's real and imaginary

It's nothing like you
            Thought it would be
It's better than sliced fucking pan
            Or meals on wheels for that matter

It's not a trick
            It's no one starving themselves
For entertainment
            David Blaine meet Bobby Sands

Good night
            It's God honest
Let's have it now
            Straight and simple

And what of the ship
       What ship
Ghost ship
       Don't say its name

Swallowed by a bottle
Why not
Why not
A blue bottle
Buzz
And floating the waves

With a message
For everyone

Arrival time
Forever and some

Museum of ice
       Of found bodies
Returned to their resting place

Thirty years?
Agreed

Here she comes
       Thank the ...

With the arrival of the iceberg
It is agreed
All poems are to be decommissioned

At last
The city
Exhales an icy breath

Mêtro

I carried your bags through the Paris Mêtro,
through the urine stench and coughing.

You limped, the two of us sea-
sawing our way to civility.

The day before, the moon had wrapped
its hands around your neck and you bled,

refused to go outside into the sun,
insisted on pulling your hair out.

The blood is magic,
a placard on the wall cried.

We were lost in Paris,
lost inside your pain.

The language made you mad;
the food, the hotel curfews, the nodding

man with the tin-foiled beer, the blocked
and leaking shower and the irate manager

plunging into our room at dawn,
chasing us down the street, shouting

'big trouble' until we came to the Mêtro again.
Dark cave of the city, skulking face

where a woman sat on a stool, her legs open,
between them a harp.

A harp between her legs in the Mêtro,
incongruous and alluring. Her face pale and serene,

white and angelic in the moving Parisian basement,
plucking gold from green, from the dark

mouth of poor anger,
making the train tracks glitter

saying *ride on me*, the strings
quivering, resonating in circles,

relieving us, for a moment, of our earthly binds
as if the cord that held us to the earth

in a heavenly balloon had been cut,
while the harpist's music promised a journey

large, yes, and golden, unrelated to the petty
quibbles of how best to get somewhere,

a journey deserving and hard, promising
a bright exit into something else,

something more intangible than the souvenir
shop kitsch, like something

in the way the mime moved outside the Louvre,
even as we were rising,

something that made you sigh and drop your last
few francs, as the landscape wavered beneath us,

into the tattered old cap
that lay peaceably at his feet.

Ode to a Badger

us in a dirt mirror
a lurching likeness

bearded Hyde
keeps to himself

comes out late at night
hectic digger of sullen dreams

elder uncle
horatian headache

secret carnivore
has claws   can kill

gnaws on bark
scared his face white

his laugh he lost
in his throat

little gorilla
with soot-saddened eyes

feasts on roots
and moonlight

there was always one
around the house

white-faced
black-striped

why you so moody
sniffed the sunrise

and swallowed the sun
badger   baritone of loneliness

hoarse barker
tired of anything bright

angry dog
gorged on the whimsical

rabbit big weasel
coughing grumpster

querulous mole
big brother to the moon

nostalgic for blood and fever
shakes his head at ignited cats

once he heard the lark
now there is nothing

if you meet a dead relative
in one of these setts

sniff and move on
no point in mourning

king of charred hearts
and proud of it

crooked smiling minister
of the unrequited

sorry bear
closing your eyes to colour

clandestine neighbour
not unlike ourselves

when in fear
secretes repugnant scents

characteristic of the weasel family
brother to the skunk

Prayer

Once while waiting for a flight, I took
the underground tour of Seattle.
Starting inside Doc Maynard's Public House,
a restored 1890s saloon, the journey

took us through the subterranean city
and into the past where hollow street
sidewalks, old gas light fixtures and
wooden pipes crumbled with time.

Afterwards I sat in a café and drank
coffee. A mother and daughter
approached and asked could they sit
at the table. They introduced themselves.

Baptists from Texas. The daughter, a pretty
blonde girl, talked about her hopes
for marriage and disparaged her mother's
display of homophobia directed at our waiter.

She's old fashioned, she said.
The mother mumbled her own objections.
Before their food came, they held hands
and asked me to join them in saying

a prayer. My hands were taken by each
one of them and the mother prayed
aloud and thanked the Lord for the food
before us and my own safe journey.

When we had eaten, they drove me to the airport,
where I waited and thought about how
the mind has it own dark caverns and when
late at night I walk through them

to inspect their junk and clutter,
their beauty and sadness, I'm conscious
of the toll, something greater than Doc
Maynard's or the merchants who

carried on business in the lowest floors
of buildings that survived the great fire.
I think of the pedestrians who continued
to use the underground sidewalks

and of the homeless who gathered there,
those who gambled, smoked opium
or drank alcohol during prohibition times:
all banished now to the light and lurid world

where the blood still beats in America's
dark heart for me and for those who
take a stranger's hands in theirs and pray
with the certitude of the saved and forgiven.

Waiting

people are all talk
there's a detour of traffic
the Guards have the street cordoned off
the commotion centres around a bin

it is Sunday
the fast food restaurants are open
but empty
everyone is here

the suicides the joy-riders
the shirtless fiddle player
the aggrieved civil servant
a hunger striker

who left his office
only to return an hour later
to a sign which read
OUT TO LUNCH

who'd want to blow up a town
like this someone says
the girl who said she was pregnant
makes an appearance

you couldn't call it exile
living here
when all is said
and nothing done

we're all waiting
for the bomb to explode
and it doesn't
well how are you

not a loss on me
the girl who said she was pregnant
has disappeared
it's a false alarm

a scare
the rumour machine
is out campaigning
and the town goes on

talking to itself
how it also ran
could have made the mark
could have been a contender

some of us don't want to go home
some want action
or entertainment
it starts to rain

and in the downpour's music
an echo of *if onlys*
scuttles down the gutter
and falls into the drain

Longford, the Wind

this is the kind of night you could write
write a poem if you had a mind to

the kind of night sleepless night
where the wind is tearing the world apart

lifting the Camlin river from its banks
the kind of night you could write yes anything

if only the stars had not been done away with
you could write yes about sleep

how it had walked away on you
or how she touched your hand

simply touched your hand
your heart like a fish out of water

maybe you'd write something like that
but you don't you're still lying

in the darkness and the wind
the wind is uprooting everything around you

your neighbours all five floors of them below you
the cinema across the road the abattoir and its stench

the bottles breaking in the bottle bank and all the poems
of Sean Cahill Noel Monahan and Rose Moran all of it

turning to dust tumbling away with Corlea bog
yes it's the kind of night you could write any of this

and get away with it you could write for example
Padraic Colum is walking down Ballymahon Street

yes anything is possible
the kind of blissful imaginings

insomnia brings
Colum when he wasn't singing a Hawai'ian song

could serve as the minstrel to carry the message
of how you'd love this girl

by now the wind has swept the possibility
of morning away so really you need to hurry

yes tonight is the kind of night
you could write what you liked

but you can't get from the bed so you can't write
I've loved you these three nights

because the wind it has you
paralysed and your heart is like a fish

out of water your breathing hardly breathing
penless dark you can't but imagine

you could write write a poem
which said the world is ending quickly

hold out your hand before the stars
are unscrewed before the moon is unplugged

before we are blown away
say your goodbyes go on write

something like tonight is the kind of night
the sea calls out to all souls shipwrecked

or not tonight you could write about the armada
and the drowning of the saints you could write

it's the kind of night ships are sinking and souls
are lost or like the day I took a wrong turn and found

myself in Ballinamuck yes a night where ghosts
walk again penless dark paralytic breathing hardly

breathing and there isn't long before it'll take
you too I'll need to get to you

or you'll need to find your way here because
the wind has plans and I've no spells or poems

to do away with it though if I did
I'd write you here I'd write a poem

which made you flesh and blood beside me
my heart like a fish out of water

breathing hardly breathing and then god help us
the wind could do its handiwork

could do what it wanted could take us body
and soul away acquiescent in its cold self-effacing grasp

my last poem
Longford, 2002

turn the television off
take the phone from its hook
light a candle
and close your eyes

what is it you wanted
what did you   *long for*

you smile at the letters
writing them where you are

the missing 'd'
let it be for 'directive'

remind yourself who it is you wanted to be

a bedroom   a reunion
Gorecki's Symphony of Sadness
at least our bodies still know each other
the only words you remember from that awful time

the 'd' the missing 'd'
let it be for 'desire'

who is it you used to be
who is it you've become
what is it you long for
what is it you desire

you're tired of being alone
of fighting with yourself

your heart you imagine
is a city
desire has made it old
its walls are falling
its bridges are on fire
there's a rumour of war

you long to be beloved
and for the right words
to keep you there
that is all

The Lady with the Coronet of Jasmine

I saw her again today.
Graceful in her poverty,
elegant. Her lips a luscious

sanguine escape. A bright
exit. Her tilted head,
diffident, but proud.

She passed me and I
smelt the fleshly odour
of temptation, heavy

in the air, eager to cling
to me. Her reckless smile
unhinging my composure.

But it cannot be.
It cannot.
It must be that my retirement

from public office is
making me drowsy,
like a summer bee

gorged on honey.
In actuality, it is twenty
years since I have seen her.

A man of my age
should not be given over to fancy,
to frenetic breaths

and tremblings. A man
of my age who at the start
of the century

heard the guns
from Edinburgh Castle
fire announcing

the abdication
of Napoleon and lived
to the end of the century,

I am ripe, and heard
his own voice,
by then a scant baritone

echo of what it once
had been, recorded by
the telephone, should not

indulge in flighty reminiscences.
And yet, memory trawls
my conscious thoughts back

to her, inevitably,
magnetically so.
And should I be so surprised?

A man, that is all I am,
a simple, imperfect man,
a man with a name of more portentousness

than pragmatism. William
Gladstone, a name, a gasp.
I say it to myself and it is

the name of a stranger.
I garden, try to remain calm.
I should make my peace.

But there she is.
In the soil as my fingers dig
for the flowers, there she is

haunting me from the past.
Emily Fenn was to be my saving
grace. An Irish peasant

from the wily shorn land
of Connemara in the West.
Wan refugee from the blighted

island next door. Alone, insomniac
walking the streets and keeping
company with other ladies

of the night.
I won't mince my words:
she was a prostitute

and I tried to save her, to rescue her
like so many other girls.
The grimy dirt of night fell around us.

Her voice was soft, plangent
like waves falling onto a shingled beach.
She mistook me for the wrong kind

of gentleman the first time I met her,
entreated me to the squalid
room she shared.

Her words were timid,
frail like chipped wood.
The misunderstanding over

we talked about her redemption.
I encouraged her to stay
at the House of Mercy

on Clewer and Rose Street in Soho.
But after a week she came back
and said she didn't want to be

locked away, that she would
have committed suicide had she stayed.
I calmed her, sat her down.

We entertained long conversations.
I read her Tennyson, which she confessed
to being much impressed by. Indeed

her very shape seemed to waver
in the candle flame, and so great
was her sincerity and enthusiasm

in this regard that I actually
gave her my signed copy of *Idylls*
and within a week she had memorised

large sections of it.
Another day.
It is no good: the calendar is

wearing me away and I can think
of nothing else, but her.
I confess, I went out of duty,

but also out of need.
Light falling on her hands,
elegant and white. My desires grew.

I sought her out. The desire
I felt when I walked the shoddy streets
of London was calamitous.

It seethed in me;
it burned, raged, galloped, slammed,
transported me into all manner

of reverie. Woman. I wanted to enter,
possess, raze and rebuild your
mysterious form, to enter

your hypnotic realm.
Emily, you represented to me
all the beautiful possibilities

of life and I courted evil
only to overcome it. I went
to her again and again and

because of the hardships she
had endured and the tales of hunger
and desperation she told of her native land,

to say hardship would be an injustice,
it was misery what she described
and all the more so for the unpleading manner

in which she relayed the story of her life,
as if such privation was itself
what God had deemed her and her own

worthy of. Six brothers, three sisters.
Her mother dead. I can hear her voice.
I am happier here, she'd say.

Though, I don't feel like the same person.
I feel like a completely different person.
And eventually I would leave after talking

for so long with the grubby feeling of money
in my hands. My garden does not need
my tending. I sit. Foolishly, I read.

My mind is moidered.
The words on the page are a weak echo
of the literature I once read.

Books with impure passages,
concealed beneath the veil
of a quite foreign medium,

so I drank the poison, sinfully
because understanding was thus hidden
by a cloud—I have stained my memory

and my soul—which may it please God
to cleanse me, as I have need.
I have read sinfully, although with disgust,

under the pretext of hunting
soberly for what was innocent.
And though today, I read the good book,

Corinthians 10, I am still afflicted
with too many memories.
I read, 'No temptation has seized you

except what is common to man.
And God is faithful; he will not let you
be tempted beyond what you can bear.

But when you are tempted,
he will also provide a way out
so that you can stand up under it.'

But Lord, this is more than I can bear.
Where are you? Answer my prayers.
When I walk those streets again,

admittedly a good deal slower,
I see her. I know it is not her,
but some likeness, some young fresh face

with a halo of jasmine. My mind
is playing tricks. And for a moment
I am happy. I think of the day

she sat for the painting my friend Dyce
composed of her, how he made her
immortal, pure, clean, after

my avaricious attacks of desire.
She was angelic, fine, the fond
glow from her cheeks forgiving me

and when he asked me to place
on her the coronet of jasmine,
I felt all the humility of a disciple.

The incredulity of Saint Thomas
with his fingers seeking out
the cave of flesh in His chest.

Yes. And yet, I suppose I felt
the guilt of Pontius Pilate.
But what grace the painting lent me.

For in it, she is gazing at me,
the missing subject, the beloved.
And yet, this is the chief burden

of my soul, rending it
to a ragged status. Desire
is gone. Mnemosyne

has chosen her to be my muse.
My wife Catherine is here,
all my loved ones. And yet...

And yet I remember returning home
time and time again to scourge myself.
The skin on my back blistered and bled

like a map of my misdeeds.
I did not tend to those wounds.
My penance was pain, physical,

self-inflicted, hopeless pain.
Even today I went to find her.
But of course, she was not there.

Only the weak resemblances I am
afraid to converse with.
And if I could find her what would I say?

Our friendship lasted but a year,
before she made her way to America.
Of course, I should have written.

She is surely living a powerful life.
How can I depart this stage
with no fond thought of those around me,

only the desperate recollections
of a short wild passion?
Coded diaries. And yet,

I think I loved her. What awful
headaches I've had today.
I go about my chores with the lethargy

of the old. I sit in the dark
to quell the pain in my head.
And now I have oral hallucinations

to contend with too. My loved ones
turn around me and weep
as if my condition is something

they can do anything about.
The redemption of these poor creatures,
that's what I wanted, now it is my own

salvation that is necessary.
I have set down a black mark
against this day, like so many others.

Give me penance, O Lord, worthy of my sins.
Tomorrow is Sunday.
What kind of atonement can He conjure?

Will He take this emblazoned image
from my mind? As if the woman
with the coronet of jasmine was a curse.

What penance will You find for me?
How will I move from this purgatorial
conflagration? And, Lord God, do I deserve to?

Map Lover
for Aoife

you will gaze
at a map on a wall
a map of intersecting streets

of a city
you have or have not
visited that may or may not

exist
you will gaze
inspect and study fondly

the oldest
and rarest of maps
of Dublin too   your city

for hours
and with the same
concentration you lavish on

your music
or me because you
will look to my eyes and hands

to my lips
my body your fingers
tapping out a cadenza onto my spine

as if I too
were a map to
the conversation of our bodies

and then
bless you   you will
with all the consummation

of a map lover
always and forever
find your way to me

Thoughts Concerning the Duration of Exile
after Brecht

1.

Bang a nail into a wall?
Don't bother.
Go on, throw your coat onto the chair.
Why worry away four days?
You'll be back by tomorrow.

Leave the tree.
Why plant it in the first place?
By the time it's this high,
You'll be well out of here.

Now if anyone passes you,
Be sure to pull down your cap.
And don't bother learning some other
Language, when the news
That calls you home is written
In a more familiar tongue.

2.

Would you look at the nail
You banged into the wall?

When will you be back?

Do you know what you really think?
Writing, working for freedom.

What do you seriously think of your work?
If you really want to know,
Go and have a look at the little chestnut tree
In the courtyard,
The one you keep schlepping a can
Full of water to...

A Letter from Perfect

Dear Paul,

I hope that you're doing great wherever you are! I thought that I would be able to send out some sort of newsletter from Rantee Bay, but that will not be happening—at least not for a while. The owners came around and I was hired. At the same time four of the Thais were fired and Mr. Add manifested his position as general manager by taking control of the money. This change meant that I and all the rest had to work harder—too hard in my mind, since we no longer had time to rest between breakfast, lunch and dinner sessions. Our smiles faded and we no longer had the energy to chat to people. After a week I got myself fired for refusing to do the laundry in between a busy lunch and dinner. A few days later Tong also stopped working. I stayed in Tong's house doing some art work, making coconut coral fish. I sold some of them, sustaining myself for about two weeks on low-calorie foods. Then one day I felt that it was enough and I left the beach.

I managed to get myself to the Temple in Sadao where I took up my work carrying heavy stones—building a new Pagoda. I did some pilgrimage tours with the monks, sleeping in caves and chanting half the night until one of the monks thought that it would be better for everyone if I could start working at the monk university in Hatyai where he was studying. To my surprise I got a job teaching English to the novice monks.

I arrived in Hatyai in the first days of April and was set up in my own private room—with a bed, the first I had slept in for about three months. After a few days we took off for a week of meditation. It later turned out to be more than two weeks but I quit after one. We woke up at 3.30 a.m., and had three hours of hard physical exercise—slow walking—"walking samati"—

sitting in the Lotus position—on our knees—all for long periods of time, always chanting. This kept on for the whole day in three-hour sessions with only short breaks for breakfast, lunch and dinner. One week was enough for me.

I went back to the temple in Hatyai where I spent my time playing trumpet and helping some Chinese and Vietnamese monks with English. I am getting pretty good at playing the trumpet and my voice is getting stronger too. The school turned out to be closed for summer holidays and soon my food supply was cut, and when my last 500 bath was finished I became dependent on my monk friends—living on the alms of the alms.

It has all been very good for me and everything is still as always Perfect. The abbot told me to wait until the 16th of May when I was supposed to start work. But by the 17th nothing had happened and I borrowed some money from a monk and bought a ticket to Bangkok. I had just a few days before I got in touch with a long-lost friend living in BK some 12 years ago. I'm in BK now and my friend is treating me well. I've just been in contact with a shipping company and it doesn't seem unrealistic that I will get a job on a ship out of here in a few days. Everything that is happening to me is still according to my dreams and I recognise the scene wherever I go. My faith is stronger than ever. And I have reached further in an understanding of the world and life.

For now I have to go. I'll be in touch again soon.

Take care of yourself.

With love

Per(fect) Zetterrman

Sunday in Belize

The sun pelts us with its lazy fury and we flounder over the border, two impetuous tourists, a ridiculous pair of Pauls, an Englishman and an Irishman, a joke really or something that sounds like one, imperial or colonial, and a without a punch-line between us, giddy as we climb into the yellow school bus, edgy, expectant and awed at the three boys revolving through Spanish and their own patois and how they joke and cajole and aid a tiny drunk man with a nest of white hair to hoist a refrigerator the size of himself onto the back of the bus, giddy and a little delirious at passing the dishevelled candy-coloured houses that seem to stumble in the heat until we are finally welcomed into the capital by a stolid colonial white spire and its stopped clock like a great dull heron with no intention of taking flight or going anywhere for that matter.

It is Sunday and Sunday in the quiet dusty stone streets, streets devoid of any of Yucatan's marauding and calamitous hawksters, but with the echo of the working week and a Canadian hiker who tells us how his travelling companion has stolen his stuff and sold it for smack. We shrug and are followed by a gangly man shaking and swerving on a child's bicycle. He doesn't want anything, he says smiling, but he follows us nonetheless, his eyes shot through with a milky blood. We consider accommodation over a drink at the only open hotel and look out onto the stultifying sea, amazed and humbled by its plangent silence, ruined only by our stupid chatter of Uxmal, Chetzin Itza, Tulum, and the ancient symmetry and sacrifice we witnessed with all the other needy tourists. On top of one temple in Merida an American couple told us how nothing compares to the Great Wall of China.

There is that to contend with and of course all the talk of whore-houses where my English friend had left me stuttering my apologies, my condescending condolences actually, something about not wanting to catch the clap, to the bemused friend of the woman he was off with. We leave the bar, the sun sinks in its reluctant way and we walk through the narrow streets of Belize far from any of my make-shift homes, or ideas of home, rambling and arguing about what we should do and where we should go when there comes from behind us a dark stream of running boys, followed by five or six sudden shadows, a silhouetted pack of dogs, leashed and growling, a mangy mess gradually, majestically almost slipping past the boys and bearing them towards the crossroads where another canine lies idling, a dumb black prince of the Sunday alley, loafing languidly and looking up, as if in slow motion, to see the other dogs racing toward it, limbering to its unsteady legs to welcome them.

We stop. The dog is set upon. Teeth sink into its flesh and tear at its sinews. Its cries fly out of the dim alley like a thousand starving seagulls. The leashes dance in the bloody sunset. A girl runs from a house. Watched by lazy eyes, she beats the dogs with a stick. She swings furiously. She swings silently until at last the boys pick their leashes from the air and pry their pets from the whining creature that lies lopsided and bleeding on the crossroads, and together they scamper away so that everything looks as it did a couple of minutes before when we had ventured down this one lone street, but that a girl is standing panting with a stick in her hand which holds her up now like a crutch, and the dog that had been soaking up the day's last sun is lying instead with its limbs torn, licking madly at its wounds and whimpering like a small child, a small human child.

Variation on the word 'love'

In these dreams
I always used to be an observer
but now things are happening
and I'm part of it

one of my friends dies in a parachute
in the ice

and there is a horse with rooms
cold medical rooms
a secret corridor

I'm scared sometimes
of the unexplored caverns of the mind
its otherworldliness
its strange calendar of back to where
you've never been
its dream logic

I would like to love you
in another time
say Berlin 1923
when Brecht is prowling under the lindens

I would like to love you
which may not happen
I would like to make love to you
to be beloved
and haunt your dreams

but the dream is like a film
made up of shots discarded
on the cutting room floor

I wonder what people mean
when they say silence
what comes with it
must also mean the end of voices

today it is snowing
and the afternoon is a bruised twilight

I have decided the following:
Berlin is a good idea
1923 or no
life may be but a dream
but love is a dream
that silence and snow are one and the same
especially if you find yourself
lying in a field and someone
is calling out your name
and it's snowing
but it's not your name
and something in the wind
as it makes its way through the grass
you are lost in
finds you
so that when you stand with your head
finally empty
you'll recognise the clouds
and the landscape they shadow

on the avenue of the portal of angels # 7

tongues turn to dust
history to the wall

you are filled with ghosts
of the lives you never lived

in a dream
there is a time
predestined
for you to die

you are fighting
struggling
the dream says
'wrankling'
with a woman
in black

behind her someone
you know
(barely)
waits
with a gun

the next night
your mouth is full of glass
here now never
shadows on the wall
your face its outline
others too
memory's echo
a picture over
an empty fireplace

of the German
here now never
a candle
a bulb no shade

alone again
with ghosts

time waits:

your move

.

Lightning Source UK Ltd.
Milton Keynes UK
UKOW05f1042120813

215232UK00001B/4/A